The Physician's Guide to Achieving Financial Freedom

By Jay E. Hochheiser, CFP®

This material contains the current opinions of the author but not necessarily those of Guardian, its subsidiaries, agents and such opinions are subject to change without notice. Opinions, estimates, forecasts, and statements of financial market trends that are based on current market conditions constitute the author's judgment. The information provided here is believed to be reliable but should not be assumed to be accurate or complete. References to specific securities, asset classes and financial markets are for illustrative purposes only and do not constitute a solicitation, offer or recommendation to purchase or sell a security.

Copyright © 2014 Jay Hochheiser, CFP®
All rights reserved.
ISBN-10: 1502583313
ISBN-13: 978-1502583314

The Physician's Guide to Achieving Financial Freedom

How secure is your life's work?

Are you fully protected from losses from life's uncertainties?

When is the last time you had a second opinion?

Are you organized to pay the least amount of taxes over your lifetime?

When is the last time all of your advisors were in the room with you talking about you?

What if you could increase financial security for your lifetime and the lifetime of your children?

Will your financial plan be successful under every possible circumstance?

Jay E. Hochheiser, CFP®

Dedicated to my wonderful wife Jill--without whose help and support my life is not possible.

And to my two amazing children, Lee and Lauren; I couldn't imagine life without them.

The amazing love we share inspires me and fuels my passion to be sure other families are truly protected and secure.

Table of Contents

Introduction	7
Chapter 1. Why Your Financial Freedom Is Susceptible to a Fracture	9
Chapter 2. Cash Flow Is King	17
Chapter 3. Protecting the Precious	20
Chapter 4. The Four Financial Stages of Your Life	35
Chapter 5. The Mortgage Clinical Trial	39
Chapter 6. The Taxability MRI	46
Chapter 7. The Three Pools of Money	53
Chapter 8. Look for the Exits Before You Enter	58
Chapter 9. Diagnosing the Future of Your Estate	65
Chapter 10. Does Charity Begin at Home or Not	74
Chapter 11. How Would You Describe YOUR Advisory Team?	76

Chapter 12. The Ideal Financial Plan   79

Chapter 13. A Worry Free Retirement   82

Chapter 14. The Choice Is...There Is No
Choice   84

Chapter 15. Advance to The Financial
Freedom Experience®   88

Acknowledgements   90

About Jay E. Hochheiser, CFP®   91

Introduction

November 2014
Woodbury, NY

Over my 31 years in the financial services industry I have seen so many physicians often make the wrong financial decisions. Some of these wrong financial decisions are not major and will not derail a physician's ability to retire comfortably or enjoy a nice life; others could be lifestyle altering.

Many times a wrong financial decision could be the difference in hundreds of thousands or possibly even millions of dollars over your lifetime.

As I have been sharing these efficient strategies and my philosophy to help physicians over the last 31 years, I thought a book highlighting some of the ways to pay less taxes over your lifetime, along with capturing creative opportunities to have more money and avoid many financial mistakes could be dramatically helpful to so many. This book is a result of that idea.

I hope this book provides you with more education and understanding so it can help change your way of thinking about the best steps to achieve financial freedom. Financial freedom is not only about the destination but it is also about the journey.

I hope you gain encouragement to see where you can enhance the value of your resources so you can enjoy a better life for you and your family not only in retirement but in all financial stages of your life.

This way you may experience a greater sense of security, and less stress all along the way.

Regards,

Jay E. Hochheiser, CFP®

Chapter 1

Why Your Financial Freedom Is Susceptible to a Fracture

Today we live in a world where there's an overabundance of information; the internet, excessive amounts of business & finance TV shows, tons of financial magazines, radio shows and more white papers then there may be actual trees left.

So knowing which strategies and financial products are best for your particular situation is a daunting task at best. Let alone knowing to what extent you should allocate your resources to fund that multitude of products and strategies.

A major problem today is that many successful physicians may be listening to what general advice the media recommends to the masses. These TV and radio shows are designed to give out cookie cutter advice and information. Generally they are really there for their entertainment value. That's what TV and radio is all about, getting you to tune in. Normally all of this advice is given in broad terms without any context for what the physician's own personal situation may be.

What I find pretty scary today is that if you earn over $116,623 in this country, you are in the top 10% of all U.S. household incomes. If you earn over $161,579, you are in the top 5% of U.S. household incomes, and if you earn over $343,926 you are in the top 1% of U.S. household incomes.

Today 90% of the wealth in this country is owned by 10% of the people.

Defining "Wealthy" in the United States

There's an old saying that the wealthy are people who earn or own more than you. From a personal perspective, this may be true; our definition of wealth is relative to our standard of comparison. (As NBC reporter Robert Frank writes in an August 27, 2012, commentary, "I often hear from older millionaires in Palm Beach or Carmel who insist that $8 million is not 'rich' where they live.") Setting aside subjective standards, here are some metrics for the definition and distribution of wealth in the United States.

Annual Income

One of the ways to measure wealth is by annual income. The Internal Revenue Service provides annual income reports based on individual tax returns. Usually the figure used is Adjusted Gross Income (AGI). The most recent data comes from 2010 had more than $34,338. This means that half of all Americans in 2010 had more than $34388 in AGI and half had less. Those above the median threshold are considered in the "top 50% of all earners," and this group comprised 67.5 million households. The table below (using IRS data in a December 2012 Kiplinger's worksheet) shows the AGI threshold for each level of earners:

To be in the...	Your 2010 AGI must be at least...	Number of households
Top 50%	$34,388	67.5 million
Top 25%	$69,126	33.8 million
Top 10%	$116.623	13.5 million
Top 5%	$161,579	6.8 million
Top 1%	$343,926	1.4 million

In the most assessments, the top 1 percent of all earners qualify for designation as "wealthy." Given the likelihood that adjusted incomes have increased a bit since 2010, it is reasonable to assert that any household with an adjusted gross income over $400,000 can be considered wealthy. (Coincidentally, the recent increase in marginal income tax rates to 39.6% from 35% affects single filers with AGIs in excess of $400,000, with a threshold of $450,000 for joint filers).

So, if you and I went into the financial magazine or media business and we were producing publications, or TV and radio shows for investment or financial advice, would we want to appeal to the 99% of the population or just 1% of the population to buy our magazines, or tune in to our TV and radio shows? Of course we would want the biggest population as a target audience for our business.

The good news is that this book is aimed at helping the 1% have more money, more security and more financial balance.

Most of the information and advice that is out there and that is preached is aimed at the 99% of U.S. households, and much of that may or may not be relevant to the physician making $500,000, $1,000,000 or $2,000,000 per year. It may help the person making $50,000, or maybe even $100,000 per year who is living in a low taxed, low cost of living state and who probably is not going to build up multi-million dollars of wealth over his or her lifetime.

As I have mentioned there is a glut of information available today, but getting solid reliable information about how money and investments really work may be hard to come by. You have so many opinions and chatter. Much of this is by non-credentialed "experts" telling you how to handle your family's finances, to me that's a scary thought.

I totally question the ability for a lot of that information that is generally out there to improve the lives of the physicians who are earning in the top 1% or top .5% of U.S. households. Those physicians are paying a boatload in taxes now and are building wealth so they are not poor in retirement but have the resources to have an amazing lifestyle not only now, but for their entire lifetime.

With all of this information and misinformation out there, and the fact that it is not aimed at the successful physician adds to the complexity of "what should I do?"

If what you knew to be true, turned out not to be true when would you want to find out?

Next you have your emotions and your spouse's emotions about money and family security. Most of the goals and dreams of the members of your family take money. Will you have enough to accomplish these things and how do you and your spouse handle losses or disappointments. Clearly there is no room here to base your financial decisions on opinion or hype.

Another factor not to be overlooked is the fact that the government keeps changing the tax laws. What was good for you at one time now may not work so well. They keep changing the rules, and your job and the job of your advisors are to keep up with that and make all the necessary adjustments.

How often does that seem to happen?

Let's not forget as well that the financial institutions keep trying to figure out more ways to get more of your money in their control so they can use it to make more money for themselves. (velocity of money to be explained later) It's a challenge to keep pace with an ever changing financial landscape as well.

Another reason that achieving financial freedom may be susceptible to a fracture is how many physicians tend to buy different financial products from different people, at different points of time. Some products they may have invested in based on hype, their neighbors opinion or something that they read. It may be a harmful product or strategy and they might not fully recover from that, or their financial freedom may not be what it could've been had they had a solution that was custom tailored for their particular situation.

So, what ends up happening is you end up owning all of this "stuff" and there is no coordination or integration of all the financial products and strategies you own. It may resemble a junk drawer if you will.

There may be no overall plan and the successful physician's financial life may be kind of a "junk drawer". As a result, they have some financial products and strategies which may be ok, and some that may not be efficient and who knows what resources they may be wasting or opportunities they may not be taking advantage of. I see this all of the time, it's extremely common.

Due to the physician's crazy busy schedule these days they have no time to really deal with this, and quite honestly they may not have the skill set, technology or even the desire to check everything out properly to be sure their financial strategies are effectively working together and in line with their vision of success.

In my over thirty years of experience in financial services I have found that there is also most often a major lack in coordination among the physician's advisors as well. Usually there are a multitude of advisors each working independently in their own cocoon without perhaps a coordinated view of your big picture.

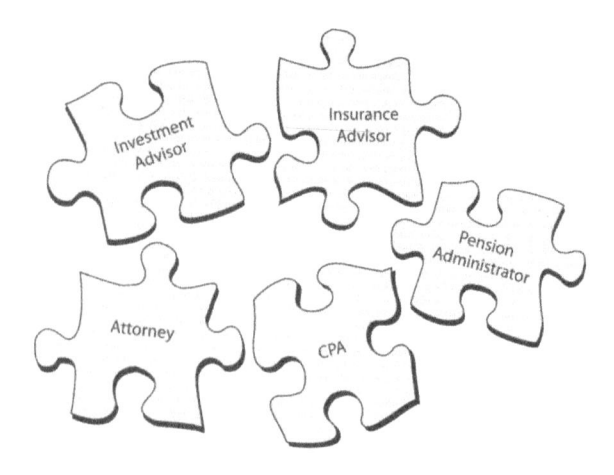

I always like to ask "**When's the last time all of your advisors were in the room with you, talking about you?**"

Usually the answer is "never."

In order for a physician to be truly successful I feel you need to have a great advisory team. There needs to be coordination not only with products and strategies you may be employing but also coordination among advisors.

Another challenge for a successful physician may be finding an advisor they can trust in a non-trusting world; finding an advisor who looks holistically at their big picture and not just with an agenda of selling their particular product. It may be challenging for them to find an advisor who they can build a long-term trusting relationship with who has the big picture covered.

Today another huge issue for physicians is that the business of medicine has become almost as important as medicine itself. The modern day physician is very bogged down with new administrative procedures that need to be done as well as different systems that may be required in order to get paid. Medical reimbursements from insurance companies and Medicare payments are always changing. You need to hire more staff members to handle some of those new administrative procedures that have become mandatory to collect money and make sure you get paid properly and you need to give those staff members' salaries, bonus plans and benefits.

Then lastly, who's looking out for the physician twenty years down the road to see how all of this is going to work out?

What does it all mean?

How are you going to best utilize the resources that you have built?

Are you going to get hammered in taxes later and should you be planning for that now?

What is your vision in five years, ten years, and twenty years' time?

Most advisors only focus on today, or possibly tomorrow. They are not looking down the road to see how the physician is going to access the wealth that they're building in an efficient manner. Many say, "don't worry about later until later". But later comes much quicker than you think, and you may lose creative options by not being future focused.

We'll address this later in the book.

So, if you have any of these questions or concerns I encourage you to read on and hopefully get a few new ideas and some additional knowledge that could make a big impact in your life and in the lives of your family forever.

Chapter 2

Cash Flow Is King

You have probably heard that cash is king, but I like to say cash flow is king!

The first basic elements of any sound financial plan are budgeting and saving.

I feel most physicians should be saving 20% to 25% of their gross income. The bare minimum is 15% of gross income. That's your income after your business and practice expenses are deducted from gross revenue, but before personal income taxes.

Depending on where you are in your career and how you've been doing with saving money for the long term would dictate 20% versus 25%. For someone who's new in their practice and they get on track saving 20% right out of the gate is very good. If someone is more established in their career and has not built the kind of wealth they should have along the way, they may need to go up to 25%. If you are in an area of healthcare with more uncertainty for what your income's going to be in the near future, you really want to be hitting that 25% number or even a little higher if possible. I realize that may seem to be a lot for many physicians today...

I know this can be challenging, but I think it's fundamental to achieving financial freedom. One of the ways to do that is to have a budget and to make financial decisions consciously so you know what you are spending and where your money is going. Let's say someone is spending a lot in one area of their life but they deem it of value, well then that's fine. When we have clients go through an exercise of completing a cash flow worksheet many times the physicians are shocked to find they are spending so much on "x", and they have no problems reducing that amount because they feel it's not worth it for them.

It's vital to know what you are spending your money on if you really want to save more. Then you can prioritize your cash flow decisions.

Paying yourself first is one of the most basic financial fundamentals but a lot of people seem to overlook it.

The more you make, the more you spend. If you pay yourself first; you'll be assured of putting money away for you and your family before you pay all your other bills. Automating your savings is one of the major keys to financial freedom, and the great thing is, with today's technology it is easier than ever. By automating your savings I feel you most definitely save more money.

Automating all of your savings is the magic bullet!!

Here I am speaking to both your personal and your practice's finances. I look at it holistically. If you're saving into your pension plan, your profit sharing plan and you're saving into other investments personally. It all counts. It's the cumulative total of all of your savings, however, I do not count 529's and saving funds for your children's college expenses. You can't count that because that's money that you're most likely going to use to pay for their education and not your own financial freedom. I deem that the 20% and 25% is for you and family down the road and not the children's educational expense. That's a separate savings.

Some physicians find working on a budget with their spouse to be enlightening and very helpful while others have found it painful and dreaded...

Every year and half or so my wife and I have what we call our "financial summit." Here we go through the cost of our lifestyle and modify the budget as warranted. We account for the credit card bills and we allow for different types of purchases to enjoy our life. By doing this we are able to consciously decide on the bigger items.

With a budget money just doesn't disappear like it does when you don't pay attention.

Once you're on track, it enables you to save more and have a great feeling of accomplishment. You have a handle on the inflows and outflows of your money and that's one key to achieving financial freedom. It really doesn't matter how much you make it is still always a great idea to have a handle on where all the money is going and if are you good with that or not? If you're not, then you take steps to correct it.

Some physicians make the mistake of thinking that the rate of return on their assets is more important than regular savings habits.

Nothing can replace good savings habits. They are at the forefront of any sound financial plan.

Chapter 3

Protecting The Precious

The next key to achieving financial freedom is something I call protecting the precious.

You want to be fully protected from losses from life's uncertainties.

You must protect 1st, fully and forever!

This is the foundation of your financial plan. You want to protect your income, your assets and most importantly your family. You want to have them fully protected in every way. So much of what we do every day is to enable us to enjoy our life with our family. Their security and wellbeing is of the highest priority for most of us.

There are several ways you need to properly protect yourself and your family.

One of your most important assets is your ability to go out and earn a living. Most things that physicians would like to accomplish in life for themselves and their families is based on their ability to go out and earn a living. If that stops usually so do most goals and dreams of the entire family, let alone the way of life as they know it. Your entire family's dreams, goals and aspirations are all on the breadwinner's shoulders and that weight definitely gets heavy at times. I'm sorry to remind you about all of this weight on your shoulders, but that's usually the way it is.

There are ways however to transfer many of those risks to an insurance company. That must be fully protected.

The definition of insurance is replacement value.

As an example, a lot of people will go out and buy a boat and they'll get the best boat insurance to protect their boat in case it gets stolen or sinks. They love this new boat! Meanwhile if they became disabled and couldn't work for any length of time, they would not be able to support their family. Possibly they also may not have the correct amount of life insurance to properly protect their family and who knows if their wills are up to date or even if they actually have written and signed wills...but their boat is fully insured! They don't have the right protection because maybe they feel "I won't get sick or disabled or die... that happens to others not to me."

Well, hopefully their right, but what if they are not?

Many times not having all of the right protection components in place is due to procrastination or not really knowing the best way to get all of this done correctly.

Is it worth risking much of your present financial resources and potentially much of the future financial resources you might be able to build to not have all of this properly covered? I think not.

There are so many things in life we have no control over, and cannot do anything to prevent them from occurring. Then are many things we can control and prepare for just in case. Those things really should be professionally measured and protected.

I think the smartest and safest way to deal with these is to transfer the risks as much as possible to the insurance companies.

Life insurance is very important.

There are basically 3 uses of life insurance.

The first purpose of life insurance is to make sure your beneficiaries are able to maintain their current lifestyles in the event of a premature death of a breadwinner. Life insurance provides the infusion of cash replacing all of the future income that has not yet been earned and will not be earned by either of the breadwinners. Making sure if something happened to you or your spouse that there was the right amount of life insurance to be able to protect the family so that they could continue to live as you would want them to. So that they could still have the same options in life that you would have wanted to provide for them if you or your spouse were still there.

You are actually replacing the person economically.

The proper amount of life insurance gives your family economic certainty. Why wouldn't you want that for your family?

The second purpose of life insurance is to aide in properly consuming an estate. This is lost on most people in the financial industry, advisors and consumers. We will talk more about this later in the book when we discuss exit strategies. (this is for you living in retirement). Yes, hopefully you will live and enjoy the fruits of your labor.

The third purpose of life insurance is to transfer an estate. This as well will be discussed more later in the book when we talk about estate planning. Most people miss the best ways to use life insurance to transfer an estate when you are much older and hopefully enjoying a great lifestyle in retirement.

The goal is to employ life insurance policies that can satisfy all 3 purposes, however, most life insurance products cannot do this.

What is the right amount of life insurance to have?

I have only heard this just a few times in my 30 years in financial services...I wish I had a dollar for every time I heard that.

There are countless generic random methods and formulas that are supposed to tell you how much life insurance you need to protect your family. None of them take into account anything about your personal situation such as who depends on you for financial support, and for how much. What colleges might your sons or daughters want to attend, do you have a special needs child or is there some kind of special charitable cause you would like to contribute to and support. There are so many variables that should be considered to arrive at how much life insurance is the correct amount for your family.

Unquestionably none of those one size fits all calculators could possibly provide the correct amount of life insurance for your family. Who would bear the brunt of those miss-calculations if or when something happens? Unfortunately it's your family, and they knew nothing of correct or incorrect analysis or measurements. Unfortunately if that happens they only wished there was more insurance dollars so that they could...

Could you just imagine if someone were to call in to a medical show like a Dr. Oz and say something to the effect that I banged my knee a few weeks ago and I can't walk so well since. And then the MD on the show recommends a knee replacement? Where were the x-rays and other tests and exams? Obviously that would have been malpractice had that Dr. operated and done a knee replacement without all of the tests and examinations. Now I know this analogy may seem a bit severe but I think you get the point.

At the highest end of how much life insurance you should have is that you would want full replacement value for all of the income that the breadwinner was going to earn. Remember we talked about how the definition of insurance is replacement value and that applies to life insurance as well.

That is called Human Life Value (HLV) and this is the economic term to describe what I have been discussing. This is the maximum amount of life insurance the insurance company will offer as they determine your economic value.

You are replacing the person economically.

Just like in the case of your boat sinking or being stolen you wanted full replacement value, why wouldn't you want full replacement value for your family on what you were going to earn over your lifetime? This is unquestionably the perfect amount of life insurance. I think you would want it, but you may not want to pay for it. There may be some additional answers for this when cost is discussed later.

The proper amount of life insurance helps provide your family with economic confidence about their future. Why wouldn't you want that for your family?

"It is a strange anomaly that men should be careful to insure their houses...and yet neglect to insure their lives, surely the most important of all to their families, and far more subject to loss." Benjamin Franklin

As a minimum, you should have enough life insurance to cover all of the lifestyle expense for your family, anticipated college costs not yet funded. You would want money to be there for a host of unaccounted for emergencies and unforeseen events that always seem to occur. They might occur with you or without you, and to have that cushion could mean a lot to your family.

One last perspective on life insurance that is also not commonly discussed is to have life insurance in anticipation of the following:

Death, Retirement, Transfer taxes, Benevolence (charity) and Love of Family including not only children but grandchildren as well.

There can be satisfaction that you are winning too, as you are spending and enjoying all of your money in retirement but still knowing you are providing financial security and financial options for your children and grandchildren that they otherwise would not have had.

Owning life insurance at ages 65-90 is actually and selfishly the best time to own it, but almost everybody misses that until they are 65 or 70 and then it may be too late or too expensive. Having permanent life insurance during your retirement years is a great time to own it so that other assets can be used for retirement income and the life insurance will pass down to their heirs income tax free and possibly estate tax free, if structured properly. The cash value can be accessed on a tax free basis as well, if done correctly. The financial industry, most advisors and most physicians have totally missed the boat on this.

We will talk more about this in the chapter on looking for the exits before you enter.

Your ability to go out and earn a living in your practice is your second most important asset.

I always place the family as your most important asset, but your ability to earn a living is really the next most important asset because if you can't go out and earn a living, everything else stops. You need your income covered as much as possible. As a physician you must have an "own Occupation" definition of disability insurance policy, so even if you could teach, lecture or do something else you would still get your disability benefits paid to you. Generally speaking you will not earn as much as you do now if you are not in your chosen specialty or practice. So the fact that you may or may not be able to earn something should not necessarily make you comfortable. You want to be sure if you cannot practice medicine as you are now you will get paid the disability benefits you're paying for. That simple. If something did happen and you experienced a disability for some time and you still could earn money doing something else you and your family would still welcome that income, but as we all know, you can't count on anything.

Earlier I mentioned transferring risk to the insurance company. That is something you must do here.

Here the best amount is to cover as much of your net after tax income as possible. My minimum recommendation for disability insurance is to cover all of your lifestyle costs. Your mortgages, other household expenses, school costs utilities cars etc...Don't forget food, your family still wants to eat even if you can't work. It is still really about covering all of your lifestyle expenses.

If you have that boat I was talking about and the boat was stolen or sunk you would want it replaced right? You wouldn't say, my boat was 41 feet and since it sunk I'm OK with insurance company replacing it with a 25 foot boat. That conversation would never happen.

It seems uncanny that with protecting your income and your family many people settle for so much less than full replacement value and even less then what they really need to secure their family and their lifestyle.

The next critical step of protecting the precious is having up to date wills and trusts. This is an area of such procrastination and delay. I get it. It's very hard having that discussion and agreeing with your spouse on who will be the Guardians, and who should be the trustees and so on and so forth. Guardians, trustees, and executors, sounds like lions tigers and bears oh my... It can definitely be a daunting task. However, unless you have up to date and properly drafted documents your children who are likely the most important thing in this world to you are not protected all unnecessarily. THIS MUST BE DONE ASAP!!!

Your family is the most important thing to you in the whole world; please don't put this off any longer.

A good advisor will work with you and help get you to an attorney and coordinate everything that needs to be coordinated with your estate plan and your wills.

Over the years so many physicians I have worked with had not addressed this so crucial part of protecting your family. While I am not an attorney I recommend the following:

Pick guardians who will love your children as their own. Try to take into account geography of where they live and where your extended family may be etc... I do strongly believe in having a separate trustee to have the control over the flow of money as most people are not good with money and having some checks and balances between guardians and trustees is important.

I do not endorse when children turn 18 getting their full inheritance. One fear is their immaturity at that age typically does not lend itself to the most prudent choices... such as getting a Ferrari or going to college as an extreme example.

My other fear would be first that they are not experienced with money and making sound proper financial decisions as I have seen in my practice over the years many people do not mature with money until they reach their mid-30's. Some unfortunately never mature with money... You of course would want them having funds for college, life expenses and other items, but waiting to give major chunks of their inheritance until they are older and hopefully able to handle it makes a lot of sense. You would want them to use what you have built and provided in a way to help secure their future instead of squandering it via mistakes and bad judgment.

You may want to allocate it to them in pieces as they hit certain milestones possibly like ages 27, 31 and 33 for example. I am sure your attorney can properly make recommendations in how best to structure that. Please be sure to consult with an estate planning attorney before proceeding with any wills and trusts. You just want to be sure that what you have worked hard to build is there for your children and accessed in the way you would want them to access it if you were to advise them.

After these basics of estate planning are taken care of there are some other items you may want in your documents but we will discuss them in the estate planning chapter.

We currently live in a very litigious society so you must be sure you're protected in a big way for any liabilities.

In our society it is mind boggling that someone could go into a MacDonald's, buy hot coffee, get burned and then sue MacDonald's and win... Crazy in my opinion!

Physicians are very aware of this open ended liability as they are many times targets and often sued. Nobody sues for just $1,000,000 anymore. Most lawsuits are $5 million, $10 million or more. You need to be sure to have a very large liability umbrella that picks up after your car insurance and homeowners insurance leaves off. The days of a $1,000,000 umbrella policy being the standard are long over.

Asset protection is extremely important for physicians. Protecting those assets you're working hard to save, build, and accumulate. You definitely want them protected from lawsuits and creditors. That is so critical.

I advocate that the goal is always to have maximum insurance at a minimum cost, but that doesn't always mean writing the smallest check.

Please do not be confused by that. It's about having the best protection for the best cost. You really need to be properly covered. In all aspects of these protection components, I favor having very large coverage amounts with high deductibles. You generally don't want to trade small dollars with the insurance companies because then they usually win and you usually lose.

You need to be aware of what investments and savings are creditor protected, and which are not.

All retirement accounts are generally protected from creditors because of ERISA laws. You may remember OJ Simpson was able to preserve his funds in his retirement accounts after he lost the wrongful death suit. His other assets were seized. Life insurance cash values are also exempt from creditors in many states, but it is a state by state statute. Tax-deferred annuities also offer protection in many states.

There are also other measures you can take to protect your assets. There are things such as asset protection trusts, but they are too involved to discuss here. They may be worth discussing further, depending on your particular situation.

Obviously your malpractice insurance will be the most expensive insurance you will own, but be sure to have the best coverage.

Now from a medical practice point of view protection takes on a whole new meaning!
If you're in a practice with multiple partners, it is critical to make sure that you have an up-to-date partnership agreement, a buy-sell agreement and proper funding for all of this.

You want to be certain that if something happens to you or one of your partners, the practice doesn't take a huge hit financially and you find the practice in a state of less revenue, more expenses and one less partner pulling his or her weight in the practice. That would make it much tougher to deal with both your personal overhead and the overhead of the practice.

Many times this is not dealt with properly in a practice with multiple physician partners. I have seen that recently and the broad reaching effects of this are very bad for all parties involved. There are no winners.

This is a key component to financial security, making sure that everything is taken care of and many times it's not given the proper attention it deserves, yet it could have a tremendously devastating financial impact if not properly addressed.

The goal of having all the right protection components in place is that you get through the hard times in a much better fashion, with as much of your assets intact, as much of your income as possible intact, and that your lifestyle is not dramatically, negatively impacted. I have seen many practices that were not prepared for things and they were extremely adversely affected. That is something that can and should be prevented.

You have worked so hard for so long to become a physician and build your practice. It would be a shame to have it all under attack from some things that were out of your control.

Please be sure to have the necessary items in place so it doesn't happen to you.

The last part on the protection discussion that I feel many physicians do not have properly covered is the coordination between all of the protection components.

For example, assuming I have minority aged children and I went to a great estate planning attorney and they drafted all the right legal documents to protect my family. If my wife and I were to pass away there was a minor's trust to protect the children, there was a separate trustee and guardian as I mentioned before and everything is set up correctly. Then I went to see someone to get the proper amount of life insurance in effect. Many times the life insurance agent or representative selling the insurance will ask the physician "who do you want as the beneficiary?" Then normally you might say "I guess my spouse and then my children." That's what they will put down on the application, and that is who the beneficiary becomes.

The problem is that it is not coordinated with the wills. If you and your spouse were to pass away the life insurance proceeds wouldn't go directly to the children since they are minors. It would be held up in court, the courts would then have to appoint a custodian for the funds and it would end up being everything but smooth and concise. The correct contingent beneficiary in this case should be the contingent minors trust created through the will. That would solve the whole issue.

There needs to be coordination between the attorney and the insurance person. This illustrates just one example of why the coordination of the protection components is very important. There are many more instances of where a lack of coordination could cause a backfire of unintended results.

On the subject of partners, as we have been discussing there are partnership agreements and then there are buy-sell agreements. This is all very tricky in medical practices as a non Dr. cannot own a share of a medical practice in many states. So you need to have of these details worked out preferably with a health care attorney. You want to be sure there is planning and coordination here too between the agreements you put in place and the insurance being used to fund these agreements. Many times I see a lack in coordination here that could really backfire and prevent the proper execution of your agreements.

Chapter 4

The Four Financial Stages of Your Life

Stage 1
Just Beginning Your Career, Your Family and Your Finances:

A focus on family protection and income replacement if you became sick or hurt and were unable to work. The need to cover household expenses and lifestyle expenses, to cover college funds and financial security that has yet to be accumulated.

The proper amounts of Disability Insurance Benefits and life insurance is critical to the family at this point as well as having proper wills and estate planning documents in place.

This is the time to create good savings habits and have great protection for unforeseen events. Starting the good savings habits now can put you on such a good path for the future!

Stage 2
Starting To Develop Your Career and Your Earnings:

You have begun to accumulate wealth and savings, you are now earning more money, but your lifestyle has also increased in both cost and enjoyment. Better lifestyle, nicer cars, vacations and greater future lifestyle expectations. Protection for both income replacement and family security needs has not decreased, it has actually increased with your higher level of success and yet the basic needs are still there as well.

The need for proper disability insurance and life insurance is present more than ever.

Tax planning starts to emerge as being very important as you are starting to pay more in income taxes.

The need to also protect your assets from lawsuits has become more important as you have started to accumulate wealth in various accounts. Proper attention on where you are building wealth becomes more important here as well.

Stage 3
The Establishment Phase of Your Career:

You're now feeling very good as you have built a nice life for yourself and your family. You have some real estate perhaps, a thriving practice and you are thoroughly enjoying your family and your life and the financial resources you have been building.

You are looking forward to not having to work a lot more years as the thoughts of financial freedom have begun entering your mind. You may have an eye towards retirement or slowing down a little in the next 5 to 15 years or so.

It might be time to map out some strategies of how you might use and enjoy what you have built with the least amount tax erosion. It would be great if you could maximize your income in retirement without losing sight of great ways to help your children and eventual grandchildren.

Most of the original protection elements are still considered vital along with the need to consider protecting your assets in the event of needing some type of long term care assistance or facilities, while still leaving all options open for planning, flexibility. You are starting to have thoughts about leaving a legacy in line with what your feelings and wishes may be.

The tax planning we discussed in the last stage is now even more important as you feel great pain in paying so much in taxes.

Stage 4
Enjoying Your Retirement Years:

You are now focused on your life in retirement. Having fun, deciding when and where you're going to travel, having new experiences and making sure you see the children and grandchildren a lot. You may be sure to see them for all the graduations, dance recitals and sporting events. You enjoy being able to help them financially when you think they could use some help, but maybe they are afraid to ask. You want to be able to use all the wealth you created to really get the most out of your life now and share that with the family too.

But still, when you are gone, you would want your children and grandchildren to have as much financial security as possible even though you won't be there to help guide them. They may make some financial mistakes along the way as well, maybe it's possible you can still bail them out…and it doesn't take away from the lifestyle you are enjoying right now.

What are the tools and strategies for helping you in all 4 financial stages of your life?

It is so important to have financial products and strategies in place that are able to help you in all 4 financial stages of your life.

I think a couple points here, the journey is very important as well as being able to retire as early and as comfortable as possible. Financial freedom means different things to different people. We always have a financial freedom discussion and what it means to each individual physician. Financial freedom for one physician might be when they hit 55 or 60 they could afford to retire but they choose to work just maybe at less of a fast pace. Maybe they adjust their schedule, maybe they take on less new patients, or maybe they only work a few days a week.

When you have enough money to be able to retire working becomes more enjoyable because you can wake up one day and say I'm done! I don't want to do this anymore because you have the financial resources behind you to take care of you and your family.

Chapter 5

The Mortgage Clinical Trial

Another area that I find most physicians really don't understand fully is the economics of mortgages. I call this the mortgage clinical trial. Mortgages are very misunderstood financial instruments among our society and among many successful physicians today. People go back to when mortgage rates were twelve, thirteen, fourteen percent and that was a horrible time period for mortgages because it cost so much money to finance your home. Fortunately the economics today are very different. Interest rates have been at historic lows and as we will be discussing later in the book, income tax rates seem to be on the way up and not on the way down. These economics favor home ownership and mortgages much more than in the past. Still I find many physicians don't choose the best way to finance either their primary home or a vacation home. They don't factor in all of the important variables so that the best financial and emotional decision can be reached.

Here as well the media usually doesn't give all of the variables and items to consider when making these extremely important decisions. They usually point out a few. Very often the variable they point out are how much interest am I paying, and how much interest will I save if I pay down or payoff my mortgage. They are clearly missing a lot of other facts that need to be considered. They are not looking the difference in tax savings between different mortgages and different methods of paying and prepaying your mortgage. That is such a huge issue for many physicians as we have been discussing the need for tax planning at every stage of life and in every strategy yet "the experts" never really mention this aspect to a mortgage. I find that so wrong.

Then what about the fact that your cash flow is going to be different and money not spent on the mortgage can be saved or invested and then you can make interest or growth on that money. How are they discussing and calculating that?

They are not even going there. Your cash flow is going to be very different taking out a 30 year mortgage vs. a 15 year mortgage. Your use of funds and tax deductions are all very different. They are never usually giving you enough information to be able to fully measure the economic difference between the mortgages. I find that very unfair.

Here is a story I call the mortgage clinical trial as an example of what some may have experienced over the last 10 to 15 years.

Let's call this couple John and Jane Smith. Back in 2002 John and Jane bought the house of their dreams for $1,500,000. They put down $500,000 as a down payment and then they took out a $1,000,000 mortgage. They decided to do a 15 year mortgage over the 30 year mortgage because the rate was a little lower than the thirty year and this way they would get done with the mortgage sooner. The bank also recommended pre-paying the mortgage to reduce the mortgage even sooner and save tons of money on interest. They decided to pre-pay the mortgage with $1,500 a month because they were told this is the smart thing to do.

Let's assume back in 2002 maybe they were paying five percent for the mortgage. Rates have come down since then, but let's say it was five percent. They were going along for a number of years and all is good. They're doing what they have been told is the smart thing.

Now enter the year 2008. If you might remember this was the beginning of a huge financial crisis in this country and in the world. So now it is 2009 and let's say John's income went down dramatically. His practice got restructured or, God forbid, let's say someone became disabled and they weren't making the same money.

They were now struggling with their bills and making the mortgage payment. John and Jane went to the bank and they said "we have been really good borrowers. We have never missed a mortgage payment and we have been pre-paying my mortgage every month. I bought my house for $1, 5000,000 and now I only owe about six hundred thousand dollars. Unfortunately I am not making the money I was and I need some money back out of the house." The bank looked at his current income and said they wouldn't be able to offer him a re-finance as his income was not high enough now to qualify for a mortgage under the current guidelines.

As you know back in 2009, the banks were not lending money even if you had great credit. The banks just went through all of these foreclosures and lending was so tight. They were not giving you money if you were disabled, or making less money to support the loan. You would be considered a big risk and they currently getting burned for so many loans that maybe should not have been given.

So now picture John and Jane, they can't afford their payments and all of their money has been virtually trapped in their house. They can't get a loan to get some of that money out of the house...It's a real big problem.

The only way to get money out of their house now is to sell it. They have to sell the house to get the money and now they have to uproot their family and their children and perhaps take them out of their school. The other problem John and Jane are also now facing is that their dream house that they bought for $1,500,000 now is only worth maybe $950,000 because if you remember, the housing crisis dramatically affected all real estate valuations. That's also assuming he could sell it, and the person he was selling it to could get a mortgage.

It's scary. If they sold it for $950,000 as an example, they would have a loss of over $500,000. That is a very ugly situation.

What if they did something different from the start? What if they took out a thirty year mortgage, even with a little higher interest rate, and didn't pre-pay it with the extra $1,500 a month? Instead they put the $1,500 into a very safe, low risk account. They now would get a larger tax deduction because by having a thirty year mortgage and not pre-paying it, you preserve your tax deductions.

It's funny because most physicians desperately want more tax deductions and yet many times they might be prepaying and paying down mortgages where they have a tax deduction. It doesn't always make sense right?

So now he also takes his extra tax savings from having the 30 year mortgage and not pre-paying it and puts that money into this same low risk safe account. Let's say he went along for those same 7 years and now was faced with this same situation he might have approximately $400,000 in that account. (this amount could differ widely depending on where it was invested) So if either one of them was disabled, or had a loss of income or they couldn't pay all of their bills, they now have an account to draw from and pay what they can't. They could afford to stay in house for a while and not have to uproot their family, not have to sell the house at such a big loss. They now had time on their side and could afford to wait out that horrible financial storm. Quite a different picture, isn't it?

Many people may have experienced something similar in 2008 or 2009. So much unnecessary financial ruin.

You may remember I said earlier that you must always protect against the unexpected.

You have to look at the economics of where we are today. For example, today you can get a mortgage at four or five percent. You get to deduct that mortgage interest. Maybe it costs you two and a half or three percent, that is your real cost. If you can invest money safely and make more than three percent then it might behoove you to do that.

A very big factor is that you control the money.

You have it in an account for your access, not the bank. A very important caveat to this is that if you or your spouse spend the difference in your payments and do not save it then you will not be better off. . If someone is going to go from a fifteen year mortgage to a thirty year mortgage and they're going to spend the difference of the payments and not put it away, and they don't have any discipline, or they don't have an automated savings like I mentioned earlier in the book, then they would be better off doing a fifteen year because they're going to spend the difference.

If you can develop an automated organized plan of saving, you are better off saving the difference and putting it away which means greater tax deductions, more access to the money, and more choices in your control, not in the banks. Also please note as itemized deduction phase outs have come back into play for 2013 and you may lose a portion of your itemized deductions, but the extra amount of deductions from handling your mortgages correctly you will still most likely get.

When you pay and prepay your mortgage, the bank takes that money back and then they loan it to someone for a credit card at twenty percent or a car loan at five percent or six percent. The banks create a "velocity of money" with the money they receive. That is how they make money. Using other people's money...yours. They don't produce or manufacture hard goods. It is all about velocity of money. Moving cash flows around to constantly make money on the turn of capital.

So why wouldn't you want to do the same. Use their money to earn more for yourself and receive greater tax deductions.

Are you using other people's money or are they using yours?

So much of the generic financial advisement is for the average person in this country and not for the successful physician. Some advice may still be helpful, but others may be extremely harmful. The mortgage situation is just one example of how generic advice could cause tremendous financial harm. I've helped so many physicians create a lot more wealth or lower their real costs of buying real estate by using their mortgages effectively with the same cash flow and the same assets. It could be hundreds of thousands of dollars or more over a twenty year period just by doing it the efficient way. I get really excited when I can help people do that.

Chapter 6

The Taxability MRI

Ok, so now that you are saving money and protecting the precious we can have fun and talk about wealth building! Yeah! Finally!!

Where should you put that 20-25% of your gross income you are now saving? You want to build wealth and you also may want to protect that wealth you are building to make sure the financial strategies you are employing are tax-efficient.

How much money really goes out for taxes and what's really in it for you??

We have been brainwashed as a society to adore and worship "the miracle of compound interest." Compound interest does seem like a great thing I agree, but what about the compounding of lost tax dollars that comes with it? Compounded lost tax dollars and the lost interest you would have made those dollars are a nightmare and no one is talking about it. When compounded lost tax dollars are calculated and measured almost everyone is startled and horrified at the same time.

Most physicians and their advisors do not analyze their financial strategies from an after tax perspective and that's the real world. It's about what you keep after all the taxes, fees and everything else that dilutes your "real gain". What do you really have left and what is the strategy really helping you gain?

It is mind boggling the amount of lost wealth that occurs from the effects of compounded lost tax dollars from tax inefficient strategies. It is enough to make you potentially sick to your stomach when you actually compute how much money is lost over time.

As a society we have also glorified high risk, high yielding, and high tax investments and compare them to low risk, low tax investments and then we assume away all the risk and taxes in our minds... it doesn't really work that way.

It is important to note that math is not money and money is not math.

You also have to take risk into account and the ability for you to be able to handle the ups and downs of the investment and be able to stay in it. This is important not only for you to be able to grow your money but also not to trigger taxable gains that were possibly from previous years but not yet realized. Even though your portfolio may have gone down this year, maybe it is up from 2 years ago.

The next huge factor is considering how you are going to use the money later. How are you going to access it and what are the efficiencies or inefficiencies with that? What happens later? Many physicians and their advisors miss this.

Years ago Steven Covey wrote the highly acclaimed book called, *The Seven Habits of Highly Effective People*. He said in his book that

"You begin with the end in mind."

I believe that when it comes to financial planning and financial strategies you have to look down the road to see how you are going to access your money and what the negative ramifications are going to be. You don't want to focus on just dollars on a page. You want to know how much of those funds are really going to be available for me to use net after taxes due.

I think many physicians and their advisors make the mistake of not looking at all of the factors involved. They look at one or two factors but not all of them.

Many physicians and their CPAs are big fans of setting up pension and profit sharing plans to build wealth and get very much needed current tax deductions. These types of qualified retirement plans are great tools to do just that, however not all retirement plans are designed equally. The goal is to custom design a plan or many times in our practice the right combination of plans to maximize your deductions and minimize the part of the contribution that has to go to your staff.

The importance of having an efficient design here cannot be overstated.

We see so many plans where the practice is giving too much to the staff and the physicians cost are higher than it needs to be. Or the plan is not designed to allow the physician to fully take advantage of current pension laws and get a much larger deductible contribution. This is of course a moving target and needs to be properly reviewed every year to see if there might be a more efficient design to better serve the physicians in the practice.

This is an area where we see many financial professionals fall asleep at the wheel.

The practice's employee demographics may change, incomes change and most often plan improvement can be made if someone is really on it year in and year out.

A warning about all pension, profit sharing and 401(k) type plans; It is very misleading when you get your pension or 401(k) investment statement and it says you have let's say $1,000,000 dollars in your plan. That $1,00,000 is not really all yours, because if you want to take that money, all of that would become 100% taxable and depending on your combined federal, state and possibly local tax bracket the government might want forty to forty-five percent of it. You really don't have a $1,000,000 million dollars like the paper shows you because not all of that money is yours. Everyone forgets that. They just read their statement and it says, I have x". Well you don't have a million because the minute you take the money the federal, state and your local governments says "where's mine?"Clearly the negative of pensions is that later when you are going to use and enjoy that money it is 100% taxable.

The financial industry has done some damage in this area by saying "You'll be in a lower tax bracket in retirement".

If you are in the bottom 95th percentile of all U.S. household incomes it is possible you will be in a lower tax bracket in retirement. If you are in the top 1% or higher of U.S. household incomes most likely you will not be a lower tax bracket in retirement as you are building wealth so you can enjoy your life. Hopefully that wealth you are building will be able to produce the kind of income you need to live nicely and not have you living at the poverty levels. We already discussed a lot of this mass media miss-information in chapter 1.

The second part of this discussion is very disturbing, but we need to have it anyway...
Where do you think tax rates are headed, up or down? As I wish they were heading down it is pretty apparent that the federal government along with many state and local municipalities have no money and will need to raise taxes to pay for everything.

Taxes have gone up over the last few years and some tax increases are clear and obvious while others may slip a little under the radar until you have your taxes done and want to know why you owe so much money.

The top bracket went up from 35% to 39.6% in 2013. That was obvious. The additional surtax of 3.8% may come in to play on much of your investment income, investment gains and dividends to pay for Obamacare may not have been so obvious. Many knew about it and some forgot. After all it is painful to always remember how much tax you are in essence paying. They also brought back the 3% phase out of your itemized deductions and the ability to lose the deductions for your dependents. I am not a CPA so please check with your CPA to see how all of this impacts you, but the bottom line is that we are all paying a lot more taxes these days.

All the more important that you employ various tax efficient strategies to protect your capital. Many times we see this aspect of financial planning missing. It's keeping an eye on what your real deal is, and measuring that against other strategies to see if you're doing the best for yourself and your family after taxes. Are you building money in the best places for your particular situation?

Another area where I feel the financial industry has totally mislead people is when it comes to advising on "how much money you will need in retirement".

They say "you will only need 70-80% of your working income in retirement."

Think about it. When you are on vacation from work don't you tend to spend more money?

You may play more golf, eat out more and you have a chance to do more, and most often that doing more, cost money.

I am not a shopper for sure, but when I am on vacation and I am more relaxed with extra time on my hands I can find myself shopping a little bit. And what happens when you shop? You buy stuff. That all adds up to spending more money. Face it, working prevents from you from spending more money because you simply do not have the time.

With all of this great technology new really cool things are surely going to be created and you're going to want to buy them. My parents never dreamed they would be buying cell phones, DVRs, and wireless routers in their house etc.

With where technology is going who knows what there will be, but it's going be cool and you're going to buy it and its going to cost money. That simple.

Items that you own are also going wear out and will need to be replaced. You may have grandchildren that you want to buy stuff for and take out and "spoil" them... Who knows what you are going to want to do for them and with them.

So ideally you would want to be able to leave your practice making "x" amount of dollars and walk into retirement making the same amount of money or maybe even more if possible.

Financial freedom is not taking a pay cut in retirement when you have more time to spend money.

We will talk more about this later in the book.

Chapter 7

The Three Pools of Money

The first pool is qualified money which would be all of your pension plan assets, profit sharing, 401(K), SEP, 403(b) and IRA's. Those funds are fully deductible at the time of contribution, they grow tax deferred and they are fully taxable at ordinary income tax rates at distribution time.

So many people advise to leave these assets for last. They advise to not spend them till you have to start taking minimum distributions. Their reason is that those assets are taxed, but the tax doesn't go away. These assets are always taxed, and taxed at your ordinary income tax bracket. If you remember our much earlier conversation, if you build wealth so that you have a nice life later on you will most likely not be in a lower tax bracket in retirement. The alternative is also very possible as horrible as it sounds...You could be in a higher tax bracket in retirement if the government continues to have trouble righting it's ship and you have saved and invested well over your working years. If you look below at the history on the US marginal tax rates from 1913 thru 2014 you will see that currently in 2014 they are below the average over that 101 year history. Some might feel they will go up by looking at this chart. Some may be afraid if that turns out to be the case.

How are you going to prepare for that?

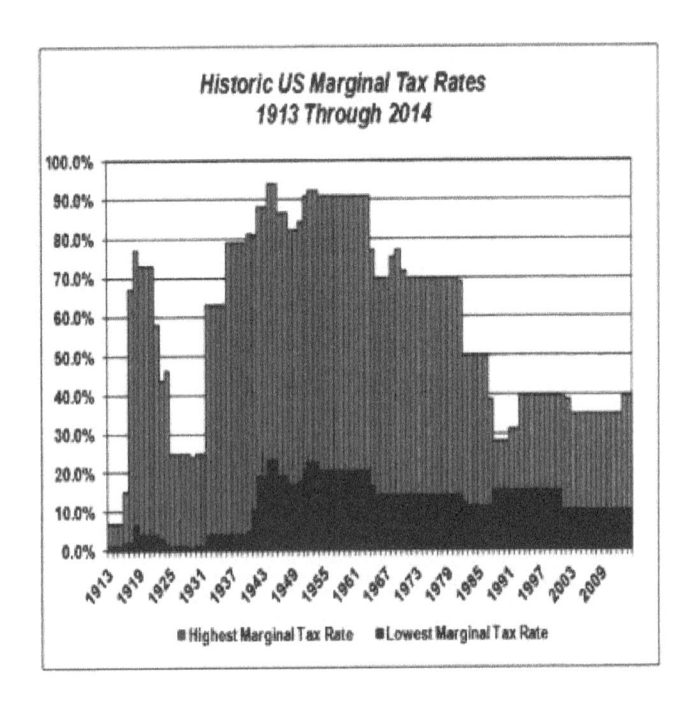

**Historic US Marginal Tax Rates
1913 Through 2014**

■ Highest Marginal Tax Rate ■ Lowest Marginal Tax Rate

So, for our example let's say you had $1,000,000 in pool #1. If you want to go and take all of that money you will pay approximately $450,000 in income taxes in our example of a combined tax rate of 45%. If you let this pool grow and compound and let's say double over some period of time to $2,000,000 while you live on your other pools of money you will also double your tax by another $450,000. These assets are taxed as ordinary income on the federal, state and local level. So you could expect to pay anywhere from 42-47% as a combined income tax rate currently. If all of your investments and savings are in pool #1 and the top tax bracket when you go to retire is up to

70% you are going to feel some major pain and experience a lot of lost capital with nowhere to turn.

The second pool is what we refer to as non¬ qualified assets. These are after tax investments in stocks, bonds, mutual funds, CDs or bank accounts. These carry with it a combination of long term capital gains taxes (which also went up in 2013) and ordinary income tax rates. Your actual combined overall tax rate will most likely vary from year to year. For our example here we will use a combined current blended tax rate of 34% that covers federal long term capital gains taxes, state and local taxes. We also had to include the 3.8% tax on investment earnings that is paying for Obama care too.

So if you had that same $1,000,000 in pool #2 and you let these assets compound and double over time as well while you spend pool #1 assets you will increase your taxes also, but if we are using a 34% combined rate you would have added approximately $340,000 of additional tax over time, not $450,000. While this example is very general it is meant to highlight the differences that are not to be ignored.

The third pool is comprised of tax free assets which would be municipal bond interest, Roth IRA's and the cash value of some life insurance policies. These assets can be accessed on a tax free basis if done correctly. You can withdraw income and have access to the cash values of whole life policies and enjoy the money without paying taxes if utilized correctly.

So what if you also had $1,000,000 in pool #3 and let this money double over time while you spent pool#1 or pool #2. You would have accumulated $2,000,000 and not have incurred any additional tax. By letting these assets grow and compound they will in most cases do this without incurring any additional taxes when you go to use the funds.

In the long run you would want the assets that compound with the least amount of taxes to have the longest compounding curve.

Please understand that this example is meant as a simplified way of looking at what is going to happen when you go to use the money you are building and start taking income or distributions. Your tax rates now and in the future definitely need to be carefully analyzed before an effective distribution plan can be properly designed. There are many variables and factors that affect these decisions.

There is a very big difference however, when looking at the most effective way to build wealth vs the most effective way to distribute wealth. Quite frankly they are at odds. You need to have financial balance to be sure you are not putting yourself in a totally precarious situation later in life when you don't want stress or anxiety.

Another very important consideration to this discussion might also be to spend the most risk based assets first in retirement as well in addition to the highest taxed assets. This is coming from a perspective of having the most security later in life when you might not deal with risk as well or you just may not have the tolerance for it.

So how are you building your pools?

Do you have a good balance?

It's definitely better to measure and address how you are building your pools as early in life as possible. There still are some strategies you can use to address this later in life if you find yourself out of balance or too exposed in any one taxable area. Different methodologies yield very different results over time. This needs to be analyzed and a plan should be put in place for the most effective distribution plan.

Under current economic conditions the most effective plan may not be what you think it is…

Chapter 8

Look For The Exits Before You Enter

In life so many things are easier to get into then they may be to get out off. Marriage is the biggest one that comes to mind.

The same can be said for real estate, private placement investments, and Real Estate Investment Trusts (REITS). Then you have some investments that you can access to but you will need to settle up with the IRS and your state and possibly local government tax agencies to pay the taxes that will be due. Those would be considered qualified money, such as all pension and profit sharing money, 401(k)s, SEP accounts, IRAs, 403(b) s and all of those tax deductible investments along with any tax deferred annuity income. We just spoke about all of this.

Most likely you're building wealth and you're probably building wealth in the different pools of money I just described.

Most people know they should diversify their assets between stocks, bonds, treasuries, and all kinds of sub categories and sub styles of investing within that, but, do most people know to diversify their assets for the different ways their money will be taxed at distribution time?

These different "pools of money" have different tax aspects to them. Some are taxed now at ordinary income tax rates, some may be taxed as long term capital gains, and many investments are taxed as a combination of both which varies from year to year.

Some investments grow tax deferred and then you pay tax when you take the money, and some are tax free at distribution time.

So how are you going to access the wealth that you are building in these "3 Pools of money", and what are the tax effects going to be?

Are you building these "3 pools of money" in some kind of balance and order?

I have seen physicians have all their money in retirement accounts like pension, profit sharing 401(k) etc. (Pool #1) While I think pension plans and retirement plans have a huge place with physicians to give them current tax deductions and to save them tax dollars today, I am in agreement with that strategy to an extent as we design, implement and manage many retirement plans for Physicians. The issue is later when you take all that money out, it is 100% taxable.

Today, if we look at income tax rates, they, they seem to be going up. The average top marginal bracket in this country from 1913 to 2013 has been around 60%. That is the average. It's currently 39.6%. It went up in 2013 from 35% to 39.6%. If you look at the federal government, your state government and all the local municipalities, they don't have enough money to pay for all the social programs and everything that needs to be done. As tax rates start to go up again, if all your money was in pool #1, (qualified money) when you go to retire and start withdrawing those funds to enjoy your life you could be in serious trouble if the top bracket is up to 70%. You might've put money away when you were in a

39.6%, 45% or 50% federal tax bracket for a deduction that year and you may be taking it out at 70%. I call this reverse tax planning.

Very importantly, I am not minimizing the power of tax deferral and even more importantly the emotional desire to save and see progress. I think that it is very important to realize that so many things in life are based on momentum. Physicians are motivated to put money into retirement plans as immediately they are saving a lot of money on current income taxes and instead it's in account with their name on it. That is a very good feeling. It is also very important to realize how that good feeling motivates you to save more and the whole thing keeps propelling you to accumulate more money. So that's all good since most physicians do not save enough. You just want to be aware of what is going to happen later on so you can try to build wealth in a good balance among your pools.

Part of the problem is the financial industry has done some damage by telling everybody you'll be in a lower bracket in retirement. The fact of the matter is if you're a successful physician, saving money and building wealth, odds are very good you will not be in a lower bracket in retirement. The goal is not to be poor in retirement. The goal is, in retirement, to actually have a better lifestyle than you had when you were working.

I think you might need one hundred or one hundred and ten percent of your money in retirement so that you can fully enjoy your life.

To do this right takes planning ahead and building in different types of options for what I call "exit strategies" in retirement. There are a few different ways to utilize these different pools you are building to maybe engineer some tax deductions in retirement. That's very exciting because when you are retiring you may not have any methods of getting tax deductions at that point.

When you're running your practice there are many types of tax deductions you might be getting. The issue is when you're retired, your children hopefully, are not dependents anymore, your mortgage may be paid off and if you're done with your practice, retired, or so forth you may not be getting the deductions there. You may be in a state of retirement but a lot of your income may taxable and you may have no deductions.

Wouldn't it be better to build in some of what I call "exit strategies" to give you tax deductions or leverage in retirement? This could give you the ability to take some money out of your retirement plan without paying the full amount of taxes that would ordinarily be due. If you could employ some complementary strategies to offer you current and/or future tax deductions they would prove to be very valuable in retirement.

How many tax-efficient levers will you be able to pull to help you in retirement?

Done correctly, you can have more security and comfort in those later years when needed, wanted and possibly critical for you to enjoy the rest of your life.

Sometimes it's not even a different product that may offer you an amazing method of getting more income or more use of your money but rather how the products can work together to produce a greater result. It's knowing how to use the different tools you may own or should own to create a better outcome.

I think that is critical. I find it advantageous to educate clients now about some of these possibilities while they are in their 40's or 50's, instead of waiting until they're in their 60's or 70's. This way you can set the stage for some of these possibilities. There are things you need to do now to make some of these tax-efficient lever available later. Don't wait until you're in your 60's or 70's to learn what you wish you knew in your 40's or 50's. That's not the best way for sure.

When it comes to taxes most people have a short term view. They are focused on paying fewer taxes today and/or paying fewer taxes next year. While I agree that's very important,

I believe the philosophy should be to pay the least amount of taxes over your lifetime.

Not just now, but later as well. Paying taxes is painful at any stage. Most physicians I know feel pain when they pay their quarterly tax estimates and maybe they feel worse on April 15th when they have to file their personal tax returns and pay whatever they may still owe in taxes. However, then they go back to work on April 16th and start to earn money again and hopefully replace what they just lost...

When you're retired or you're in your financial freedom stage of life, and you have to pay taxes you may not be working anymore to replace that money. I think that's really bad as well, in fact that may be worse. Also, down the road you may want to help family members, children and grandchildren. I am sure there are going be lots of other things you are going to want to do so you want to make sure that you have all the creative strategies available to you. Most often to really take advantage of various planning opportunities some elements may need to be in place earlier in life and unfortunately most people miss that until they are older.

There's a lot of moving parts to setting yourself up to have some of these options in retirement. This is where you need someone looking after the big picture and coordinating all financial strategies products and advisors. A quarterback if you will. You lose out if you don't have someone looking at the bigger picture and accessing what's going to happen down the road.

So, what's your plan?

As I mentioned earlier, the coordination with the protection components is important. The coordination with the wealth building and wealth distributing strategies are also very critical because you want to build wealth in the best proportion in the different pools to use them at the right times later. That requires total coordination, and again a holistic approach to understand the economics of your situation and how to best use what you have built in the most efficient order and method.

I assure you that employing different methods of distributing these pools of money at different times will definitely not yield the same results. The difference in amounts of taxes paid and income received can be quite substantial throughout your lifetime.

Chapter 9

Diagnosing the Future of Your Estate

Estate planning doesn't mean you are planning to die, or you are planning to go and give away or lock up all of your assets. Estate planning is basically putting down on paper and devising a plan for who you would like to get what and when if something happens to you, your spouse or both. In what manner over what time period with what checks and balances. You also want to be able to do that with least amount of taxes, costs and family hassles. You want to have the plan as equitable as possible, but that isn't always equal...

The goal is to keep your money where it belongs, with those you love.

The idea is to develop a plan around your wishes and it may be simple or many times it can be more complicated to have your desires and wishes carried out correctly. A huge key here to note is that how your assets are owned is critical. You may have a spectacular will drafted but if your assets are not titled correctly the will won't work... crazy right? The coordination of wills and titling of assets is absolutely critical for you wills to work the way you want.

Here too it can be challenging as the government is always changes the laws on estate taxes. The estate tax laws have been changed so many times in our nation's history. It all started in 1898 believe it or not. Then they were taxing estates greater than or equal to $10,000. Then in 1916 they taxed only estates over $50,000. The estate tax was repealed in 1926, and then reinstated in1932. Then they went back and forth on the tax rates charged and on estate values that were deemed taxable. Then they added a 15%excise taxes on having too much money in qualified pension plans that lasted until 1997. Then that tax was repealed...

In 2010 they put forth a 2 year provision to raise the allowable amount of money one could transfer without taxes to $5,000,000. In 2012 it was $5,120,000; $5,250,000 in 2013 and $5,340,000 in 2014. The number is indexed for inflation.

Do you really think it won't change again?

Another factor is that the estate tax rates and amounts of assets that avoid taxes in your state are different then the federal government and generally much lower. Many states have a $1,000,000 threshold of what is not taxable and then the state estate tax rates could be 7-15%. Most states have different taxation thresholds then the federal government and sometimes the physicians we work with were unaware of these differences.

There are several methods of being able to discount the taxable estate values of many assets you may own or acquire. Attorneys can create separate legal entities to accomplish this. You gift some shares while you still would control the assets or majority interest and the majority of the revenue. An estate planning attorney may recommend a Family Limited Partnership, or an LLC. There are a lot of different ways to do this and it could get complicated to have this done correctly... You definitely need to map everything out and then meet with a good estate planning attorney to get it right.

This is definitely not a case of one size fits all. You really need to understand the flows of assets and income in all of these potential scenarios. There are some great methods to insure that you can pass on a legacy of significance, but there are normally some types of restrictions or complications you need to be aware of.

Some mistakes you might make when thinking about estate planning:

1. You don't think you have enough money to do estate planning: As you may have seen from the chapter on protection you always need to protect who is in your life and what assets you have built or acquired.

2. Having outdated wills and trusts that may name people to be guardians, trustees or executors that you may not even talk to any more or who you may not like or trust anymore. This happens all the time, but it could become a huge problem if not fixed before something unforeseen happens.

3. Don't lock up or lose access to a lot of your money and lose the ability to use it to make more money. You really want to able to control your money and assets so you can use them to the fullest extent of their capability.

4. Don't jump on the 2nd to die life insurance bandwagon so fast. Life insurance is an integral part of most estate plans, but there are many different strategies here and they are vastly different with vastly different outcomes.

It makes so much more sense to be able to gift to your children or grandchildren later in life when you have much better idea as to how much on each particular asset you will want or need in retirement.

Gift taxes vs. Estate taxes, they are not the same and this you really need to know.

They carry the same tax rate but are vastly different in terms of transferring wealth.

You definitely want to build in options to do estate planning after the first spouse passes away.

Most people don't know there is a world of difference between estate taxes and gift taxes. Please see below where I explain the difference between an inclusive tax and an exclusive tax.

So many advanced estate planning strategies entail large changes in the way your assets are handled. It is very hard to know when you are in your 40's, 50's or even 60's what assets you will want or need when you are in your 70's, 80's or 90's. It would be guesswork at best and I feel that's no way to do planning.

We find it so much more important to build in flexibility to be able to do as much of this kind of estate planning after the first spouse passes away. Many times, when that happens you may be in your 70's or 80's and then you surely will have a much better idea of what your finances look like. Then you may know what assets you need and what assets you do not.

The other aspect of being able to do planning in this way allows you to possibly make large gifts to your children while one spouse is alive and there are many benefits to this approach. First you remove an asset from your estate at that point and then the future growth of that asset is not in your estate any longer. Your children don't have to wait till both you and your spouse are gone to possibly enjoy some the fruits of your labor, and you can see them enjoy using some of those resources for themselves and possibly your grandchildren. It can also be a great way of paying a lot less estate taxes as well.

To me, this is so much better. The problem is that 2nd to die life insurance does not give you that option. You lose all flexibility and a potential magnitude of savings or estate leveraging.

So let's take an example of Steve and Mary Jones. Let's say Steve unfortunately passes away in his 70's and Mary lives to the average of 14 years longer than her husband to her mid 80's. I will use for simplicity sake a 50% federal estate rate. At the time of your reading this the actual rate may be higher or lower depending on how many times the government has changed the rates after this book was published.

So by the time that Mary passes away in her mid 80's we will assume they had a $20,000,000 taxable estate after all credits and deductions etc…at a 50% estate tax rate their kids would pay $10, 000,000 in taxes and then inherit $10,000,000. Unfortunately the cost for their children or heirs is $10,000,000 to get $10,000,000. Painful at best…

Now some financial planners, estate planners and insurance agents say just buy $10,000,000 of 2nd to die life insurance and let that pay the tax...Well that could definitely help and would cover that tax if that is what it ended up being in 20, 30 or 40 years down the road from when they bought the policy...

What if they did something different? What if after Steve passed away, Mary realized that she could afford gift a building she owned to her children as she did not need the rental income anymore and maybe gift their family's vacation home for a total asset value of $10,000,000 now while she's alive? The gift tax in this example would be $5,000,000. Gift tax is 50% tax on the amount gifted. The same tax rate as estate taxes, but the results are very different. So in this case it cost them $15,000,000 to pass $10,000,000 of assets to their children, not the $20,000,000 in the previous example. That's $5,000,000 less than the estate taxes. Big difference, right?

Now let's bring in the insurance discussion. If Steve and Mary had bought a 2nd to die life insurance policy nothing happens after Steve dies except Mary still has to continue paying premiums and no insurance proceeds come in. After something like this happens the widows or widowers always want to know why they have to keep paying the premiums and why there's not any life insurance proceeds now...

If they had 1st to die insurance, and Steve passed away as in this example, the $10,000,000 of insurance could be used to pay the gift tax that was due in this example and Mary would only needed

$5,000,00. Then there is still $5,000,000 left that either Mary could use or even leave it in an account or in a trust if that was where the life insurance was owned. Now the future growth of that remaining $5,000,000 could be quite large and still be out of the estate if it was in a trust. Mary could also gift $20,000,000 of assets if she had it and didn't need it and just use all of the insurance to pay the gift tax. It might be nice for Mary to see her children and grandchildren benefiting from the rental income the building throws off since she didn't need it any more. Maybe she would take some of the insurance proceeds and pay for all of her grandchildren's education or help them with a house down payment.

Mary has so many options that are all good and she is under no pressure to do anything. There may be some real super strategy available at that point that wasn't available when they were drafting their wills and trusts 20, 30 or 40 years prior. Who knows?

What we do know is that options are good, and saving millions of your hard earned dollars is great! Giving more to your family and a lot less to the IRS is priceless.

It's all about having the flexibility and you get none of that flexibility with 2nd to die life insurance. You get a cheaper bill, and that's probably the only thing you will ever be happy about with it.

The goal generally is to have the best lifestyle possible and enjoy the wealth you have built and then put yourself in a position to transfer that wealth to who you want when you want with least amount of taxes and fees. I don't see how you do that without options and flexibility later on in life. There is no way to predict how you can do that 20, 30 or 40 years in advance.

Most people miss this, and all may have significantly less because of that. Many families will possess less wealth and less enjoyment of that wealth because of this.

Please look at the example below on gift tax vs. estate tax.

Passing Wealth to heirs - Inclusive versus Exclusive

Estate Tax = Inclusive	Gift Tax = Exclusive
Heirs inherit $20,000,000	Grantor gifts $10,000,000 to Heirs
Heirs pay 50% Estate Tax* ($10,000,000)	Grantor pays 50% Gift Tax ($5,000,000)
$10,000,000 net to Heirs	$10,000,000 net to Heirs
Total cost for heirs to receive $10,000,000...	Total cost for heirs to receive $10,000,000...
$20,000,000	**$15,000,000**

*Estate tax rates are subject to change -currently 40% Federal (has been as high as 55%) + your state tax rates could be anywhere from 6-8% currently

HOCHHEISER, DEUTSCH
& Company Inc

Many physicians we have worked with would like to pass along a legacy of significance and protect their wealth for not only themselves but all future generations' as well. Keeping the wealth that you have worked so hard to build in the bloodline. I call this "Bloodline Protection."

With the right methods of planning and the right advisory team you can execute a great estate plan with confidence and clarity knowing you have done the best you could for your family.

Chapter 10

Does Charity Begin at Home or Not?

There are some really great Charitable Planning strategies that can be amazing for you to employ in retirement. Some of them will give you tax deductions that may be quite large and others will reduce the value of your taxable estate or allow you to transfer more wealth with less tax and of course help some of the charities that may be close to your heart.

Many physicians have multiple charitable interests as they are focused on providing health, wellness and helping society as a whole. So it seems natural to me that if they were aware of some potentially mutually beneficial charitable strategies that could help a charity and help them have more cash flow and pay less taxes they would be all over it. In my opinion this should be discussed to see if there are charitable strategies that may be a good fit. If done correctly, usually the only one who lose is the I.R.S.

Many times the best way to be able to utilize some of these charitable planning strategies down the road is set up by different things you may employ earlier in life. Paving the way for all kinds of options and flexibility later. You may recall in chapter four where I discuss The Four Financial Stages of Your Life, and Look for The Exits Before You Enter in chapter 9. These all remind you that it's best to look ahead when trying to figure out which products and strategies will help you throughout your lifetime as much as possible. It's not just about the here and now.

Just as we discussed needing an expert trust and estate attorney earlier for your estate planning documents, here you would need the same to put the best charitable strategies in effect as well.

Chapter 11

How Would You Describe YOUR Advisory Team?

In order to for you to maximize your financial potential you cannot afford to waste any financial resources along the way. You need to be taking a Macro manager approach to oversee the big picture and be sure to have all of your advisors and financial strategies working together on your behalf and on the same page.

You need someone to take the role of the Quarterback. This person will need to get a handle on all the moving pieces and provide the coordination I have been discussing. You will also need a great CPA and a great attorney. Then once you get a 2nd opinion on all of the financial products and strategies you have been employing along the way you will get an idea of who else you want on your team. To achieve financial freedom and to maximize your wealth potential you do need to have an amazing advisory team.

As I mentioned earlier, it's about when's the last time all of your advisors were in the room with you talking about you and your family? In many cases the answer is never. In some cases there is some coordination, but is that really good enough?

Many advisors don't have the vision or the specialty of a holistic approach to guide physicians to build and distribute wealth that can be enjoyed through all financial stages of their life. That is one of the major aspects that we really focus on.

THE MACRO-MANAGER APPROACH

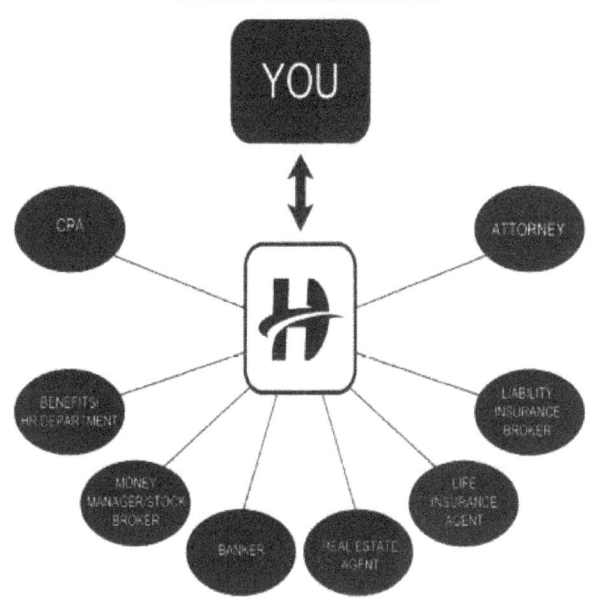

The entire team should have one focus, and that is to help you and your family the most with the least amount of time spent on your end. The team members should be working behind the scenes in your best interests and bring you in the fold to discuss strategies, recommendations and the best outcomes.

What are you currently using to measure your progress and your success?

"Progress that is measured improves; progress that is measured and reported improves exponentially."
~Dan Sullivan

The goal is to make sure that everyone's on the same page, taking care of you, and also doing what is necessary behind the scenes on your behalf in a coordinated fashion to alleviate time that you need to spend on the nitty gritty when probably it's not your first choice to do.

Chapter 12

The Ideal Financial Plan

While we don't live an ideal world I feel you should know the elements that are present in an ideal financial plan.

You have an automated systematic flow of money into the plan. Your wealth building engine needs fuel or it won't go very far. You need to be feeding your financial plan.

You have a guaranteed rate of return. It's hard to spend maybes in retirement. Having guarantees with some of your funds definitely eases stress in periods of market volatility.

You have accessibility to the money should you need or want some of it or all of it. Unforeseen events happen all the time. You don't want to be locked out of your money. It always seems to be that you need some funds when they may not be available. Call it Murphy's Law.

There would be minimum taxes on the money as it accumulates and grows. This is very important as we have discussed. The pain in paying so much in taxes is not only frustrating but the compound effect of taxes takes away boatloads of money from you and your family.

There would be minimum taxes on the money when you take it out, even bigger and more important. Having to pay taxes on money you are withdrawing in retirement is downright depressing as you will not likely earn more money to replace that lost money.

You would be able to minimize losses due to market volatility. Market volatility when withdrawing funds can cripple a financial plan. If you have analyzed or seen the effects of this you know how it can dramatically change your retirement lifestyle.

THE GUARDIAN INSURANCE & ANNUITY COMPANY, INC. (GIAC)

How Will Market Ups And Downs Affect Your Retirement?

While you can control how your investments are allocated and how much you withdraw each year, no one can predict when market highs and lows will occur. This chart shows an example of the same hypothetical investment returns during both the building (Accumulation) and the withdrawal (Distribution) phase. The results are the same while building assets but vastly different once withdrawals begin. As you can see, negative returns during the early years of a withdrawal program have serious consequences on a portfolio. Avoiding severe initial negative returns is critical to sustaining withdrawals over a long period of time.

Investment Results Before And During Retirement

Building Assets/Accumulation Phase
Withdrawals: None

Starting Value for Portfolio A and B: $100,000

Age	Portfolio A Annual Return	Portfolio A Year-End Value	Portfolio B Annual Return	Portfolio B Year-End Value
41	-9%	$90,896	19%	$119,186
42	-12%	$80,092	18%	$140,568
43	-22%	$62,391	22%	$171,715
44	14%	$71,313	-8%	$158,304
45	19%	$84,859	15%	$182,240
46	5%	$89,315	8%	$197,566
47	17%	$104,149	23%	$242,928
48	1%	$105,524	-3%	$235,512
49	-3%	$102,248	16%	$272,709
50	22%	$124,279	19%	$323,611
51	19%	$147,407	30%	$422,202
52	6%	$156,654	10%	$464,754
53	-15%	$133,644	-15%	$396,487
54	10%	$147,113	6%	$421,362
55	30%	$191,933	19%	$499,776
56	19%	$227,757	22%	$607,459
57	16%	$263,730	-3%	$588,602
58	-3%	$255,679	1%	$596,374
59	23%	$314,384	17%	$695,422
60	8%	$340,823	5%	$731,936
61	15%	$392,356	19%	$870,966
62	-8%	$361,713	14%	$995,517
63	22%	$441,861	-22%	$775,503
64	18%	$521,131	-12%	$683,328
65	19%	$621,115	-9%	$621,115
	8%	**$621,115**	**8%**	**$621,115**

No Difference in final portfolio value even though the pattern of market performance varied significantly.

Taking Withdrawals/Distribution Phase
Withdrawals: 5% of $621,115 value.
Withdrawals are adjusted for 3% annual inflation.
Starting Value for Portfolio A and B: $621,115

Age	Portfolio A Annual Return	Portfolio A Year-End Value	Portfolio B Annual Return	Portfolio B Year-End Value
66	-9%	$533,511	19%	$706,040
67	-12%	$438,111	18%	$800,716
68	-22%	$309,339	22%	$945,192
69	14%	$318,498	-8%	$837,437
70	19%	$344,042	15%	$929,104
71	5%	$326,705	8%	$971,239
72	17%	$343,183	23%	$1,157,156
73	1%	$309,520	-3%	$1,083,638
74	-3%	$260,571	16%	$1,215,450
75	22%	$276,193	19%	$1,401,794
76	19%	$285,856	30%	$1,787,126
77	6%	$260,801	10%	$1,924,257
78	-15%	$178,214	-15%	$1,597,329
79	10%	$150,570	6%	$1,651,935
80	30%	$149,467	19%	$1,912,379
81	19%	$128,982	22%	$2,276,041
82	16%	$99,518	-3%	$2,155,552
83	-3%	$45,150	1%	$2,132,685
84	23%	$2,646	17%	$2,434,017
85	8%	$0	5%	$2,507,361
86	15%	$0	19%	$2,927,542
87	-8%	$0	14%	$3,288,418
88	22%	$0	-22%	$2,502,155
89	18%	$0	-12%	$2,143,462
90	19%	$0	-9%	$1,885,183
	8%	**$0**	**8%**	**$1,885,183**

Significant Difference in how long the portfolio lasted based on the pattern of market performance.

Charts are hypothetical and for illustrative purposes only, do not represent an investment in a particular investment vehicle, and are not intended to indicate future investment results.

The plan would be self-completing in the event you became disabled and couldn't work. This would provide so much financial balance. Having something in place that does this is a huge win.

You had flexibility to adjust and change the plan when warranted or needed. The only constant in life is change. So much is always open to change in your practice, in your finances and in tax laws.

Your money is protected from creditors and as many eroding factors as possible. Between inflation, creditors and tax law changes it is critical to shelter your wealth today.

The real goal is to have your financial plan successful under every possible circumstance.

Chapter 13

A Worry Free Retirement

This is what you and your advisory team should be working towards on your behalf. That work starts now, not later as you get closer to achieving Financial Freedom. All roads should lead to this. Having a worry free retirement is your reward for working hard and planning smart. At this point it is all about having safe, reliable consistent income sources in retirement. That's what everyone wants & that's what it is supposed to be like.

The Worry-Free Retirement

Risks in Retirement

- Longevity Risk
- Propensity to Consume
- Higher Income taxes
- Market Risk/Principal Risk
- Inflation
- Lawsuit
- Unplanned events
- Running out of money as you get older
- Disabled before a chance to build enough wealth to be able to retire
- Prolonged illness
- Kids/Parents may need financial assistance
- Needing more money to live on than you thought
- Long term care expenses
- Unanticipated family needs

Ideal Goals in Retirement

- Stability
- Predictability
- Tax free income
- Contingency Plan
- Capability to create leverage
- Ease of use
- Creditor protection
- Still get some tax benefits & tax reducing strategies

It's not necessarily about how much money you have but what types of assets you have and how you can most effectively use them.

Helping To Provide Financial Freedom For Successful Professionals And Entrepreneurs — HOCHHEISER, DEUTSCH & Company Inc.

I believe you always should have this in focus and in your thoughts when making any kind if financial decisions. You and your advisory team should make it happen!

Chapter 14

The Choice Is...There Is No Choice

As we have been talking about so many uncoordinated, unsubstantiated financial products purchased over time many without accurate measurements of success. How could you possibly compare a systematic holistic process to simply purchasing a product and hope it works out?

You cannot compare. If you were to go out and buy the newest golf club let's say a new driver. It might help your game a little just because of technology and how it is helping the average golf a little bit. In reality is it is not going to drop your handicap by 5, 10 or 15 strokes... (The driver is the product)

Now let's say instead of buying that new driver, you invested in some lessons and a very good teacher worked on your swing, and improved your swing, (a process). That would have universal applications and could make a big difference in your golf game. Now, truth be told it is much easier to go out and just buy a new club than spend time in lessons and practicing... but the results are also very different.

Except buying the wrong financial products could result in much worse ramifications then a slice, a hook or hitting a ball in the water. The penalties could be much more severe with the wrong financial products or strategies.

The goal is to make your financial plan successful under any circumstance!

If taxes go up, if interest rates go down, and if the stock market crashes.

You need to protect against the unexpected while growing your wealth. I feel that can only be achieved through a process. You need a process to coordinate organize and integrate all strategies, products and advisors. The coordination allows you to have the flexibility to adjust and change the plan when it's warranted.

Our comprehensive holistic approach is called The Financial Freedom Experience®. It is comprised of 3 proven and trademarked processes all aimed at providing education on how financial products and strategies really work and helping you grow and utilize your wealth in the most tax efficient manner, and most of all protect your wealth.

How Secure is Your Life's Work?

Are you taking advantage of every opportunity in your practice to create greater personal wealth? Our Business and Professional Practice Advantage ™ process looks to do just that. You also should be integrating your personal strategies with those in your practice to create a cohesive plan. You also want to protect the interests of all key members of your practice to be sure that all families are protected now and in the future.

Have you considered what you're succession plan might be resulting in leaving a legacy that you can be proud of.

Three steps to greater wealth and security is the focus of our process called The L.I.F.E. Approach™. That stands for Lifelong Improvements for Financial Empowerment. Above all else, this unique and powerful approach helps to insure that you and your family will be protected now and forever.

We want to protect your family forever, in the event you can't.

We will analyze, test and guide you on all your present and future financial strategies, giving you the clarity to help you attain your financial goals.

At the end of the process you will feel empowered knowing you have made the right financial decisions for you and your family.

Lastly, we offer The Retirement and Estate Navigator™. Regardless of your age, it's important to take an honest and realistic look at the type of lifestyle your financial resources will provide in retirement.

The time to do that is now!

Our process will provide you with a vital step by step process to identify and test different strategies to maximize your income in retirement. Then you want to be sure to have a tax-efficient legacy plan that accomplishes your wishes.

Confidence and security comes from knowing you've finally taken the right steps.

You cannot accomplish all of this I have mentioned here and be guided through all of the complexities of today's and tomorrow's financial world without a thorough and holistic process.

Chapter 15

Advance to The Financial Freedom Experience®

Begin your financial freedom journey now!

It only takes about seventy-five minutes to get you on the road to financial freedom. We have an initial meeting that we call The Financial Freedom Design Session™. It's a meeting that we have together with you and that gets you on the road to financial freedom.

You can go to our website at www.HDCI.biz and then e-mail us and request a Financial Freedom Design Session™ and we will schedule that with you and get you started. Or you can email us at info@hdci.biz as well.

It's really a lot easier then you may think. We will educate you and guide you all along the way.

Investing seventy-five minutes could really be the difference between having security, financial balance, and enjoyment by achieving financial freedom or being frustrated by your lack of options and not harnessing the full power of your resources.

We make a huge difference in physician's lives and the lives of their family. It's something that makes us feel great about what we do. We help you be protected and we look out for you by making sure that you are doing the right things at the right times for you and your family.

We've done so much to help physicians enjoy their retirement, buy their vacation homes, protect their loved ones, send their kids to college, and do it all in an efficient format that creates the best lifestyle now and in the future for them and their families to enjoy.

I will close this book with our worthy ideal. This is what we stand for and why we do what we do. I wish you and your family all the success in life and I am hoping I was able to add to it.

Thank you.

Jay E. Hochheiser, CFP®

Our worthy ideal is to inspire and guide families to protect themselves from life's uncertainties, to safeguard and grow their wealth so they have the freedom to enjoy life with financial clarity and confidence.

Acknowledgements

I want to thank my family for their support and genuine interest in this book. I appreciate all of the relentless conversations we had about the book and their patience as it took much longer than I had hoped or expected.

I want to thank my team at Hochheiser, Deutsch & Company Inc. for all of their help with this book and all that they do for me and our clients every day. You are all so amazing at what you do and for providing me with the time to write this book. A special thank you to Katherine. You are just the best!

I also want to thank Dan Sullivan from The Strategic Coach. Without Dan and his wisdom and encouragement, this book would never have been written, or written in this century.

I owe a debt of gratitude to Rick Wollman of Empowered Mastery Consultants for all of his marketing input and help throughout the last few years. Rick, you have helped us transform our communication so everyone knows who we really are and what we really do and who we do it for. Thank you!

Lastly I want to thank Hilary Topper from HJMT Public Relations for everything she has done and everything she and her firm will continue to do to make us a successful household name.

About Jay E. Hochheiser, CFP®

Jay's primary focus is helping to inspire and guide families to protect themselves from life's uncertainties and to safeguard and grow their wealth so they have the freedom to enjoy life with financial clarity and confidence. A wealth management strategist for over 30 years, Jay specializes in overseeing the complete financial picture of successful professionals and entrepreneurs.

"I was fortunate to have found my passion early in life – helping hundreds of high-net worth clients manage their financial decisions. I look forward to continuing to do so for many more years to come."

The quotes on the back cover represent the personal views of a select group of Jay Hochheiser's clients and may not represent the experience of other clients. The opinions are not indicative of future performance or results.

Achievements

Founder and CEO of Hochheiser, Deutsch & Company, Inc.

Created numerous powerful and proven trademarked processes

Guaranteed more than $1.5 billion dollars' worth of protection for families across the country*

Receiver of numerous prestigious industry awards at the highest level

Serves on the Men's Division of the Children's Medical Fund of New York (CMF)

Favorite Quote

"The definition of insanity is doing the same thing over and over and expecting different results." Albert Einstein

---

*Total Life Insurance Coverage in force for all clients as of 10/27/2014

Jay Hochheiser, Registered Representative and Financial Advisor of Park Ave Securities LLC (PAS), 250 Crossways Park Drive, Woodbury, NY 11797. Securities products / services and advisory services are offered through PAS, a registered broker-dealer and investment advisor, 516-677-6200. Financial Representative, The Guardian Life Insurance Company of America (Guardian), New York, NY. PAS is an indirect, wholly owned subsidiary of Guardian. Hochheiser, Deutsch & Company, Inc is not an affiliate or subsidiary of PAS or Guardian. Guardian, its subsidiaries, agents or employees do not provide legal or tax advice. PAS is member of FINRA, SIPC